Kenshiro Abbe
The forgotten Budoka

Compiled by Abdul Rashid

DEDICATION

I would like to dedicate this book to the late Syd Hoare. He has made tremendous contributions to the world of martial arts up until his passing. This publication is only possible due to his relentless efforts.

CONTENTS

ACKNOWLEDGMENTS

I would like to acknowledge the following individuals:

Syd Hoare

Derek Eastman

Bill Woods

Gerry Gyngell

Teresa Reeve

ACKNOWLEDGMENTS

Special thanks to the following individuals:

Henry Ellis: *Thanks for the continuous support and contribution*

Ellis Amdur: *Thanks for sharing several photographs for this writing*

Professor Michael Belzer: *Thanks very much for the inspiration. If you had not sent me the booklet about Draeger, I would not have gotten the idea to write this*

George McCall: *Thanks for helping me in finding information*

I strongly believe that credit must be given where its due. I would like to give full credits to Syd Hoare. Presented in this booklet is his translation of an article written on Kenshiro Abbe. Many, including myself were unaware of the existence of such article. Not to mention the original Japanese writer, whose identity is still unknown, for going full length to interview the late Kenshiro Abbe, his colleagues and family.

Details of this article is quite scarce. Based on the content, it was originally written in the mid-1980s. The translation however, seemed to have been done about a decade ago, sometime in 2010. Nevertheless, a big thanks to Syd Hoare for uncovering the lost work and making it available to a wider range of audience, which can be still found on the internet.

I have always been fascinated by Kenshiro Abbe and his contribution to the world of martial arts. Despite his credentials in the martial arts, I have always felt that his name was in the shadows, alien to most people. Over the past year, along with 2 of his students, I wrote 2 books about his involvement in the United Kingdom. *"Founding of Jujutsu, Judo & Aikido in the United Kingdom"* and *"British Aikido History: The story of two pioneers from the Kenshiro Abbe era"*.

This publication, however, presents a different view of Kenshiro Abbe. It goes into detail about his early life. Particularly, his life as a Judoka. I have added in relevant photos and edited the text to make it suitable for publishing, whilst staying true to the original source as much as possible. Along with that, there is an additional contribution from one of Abbe's direct student.

I hope that the readers will enjoy this.

Abdul Rashid

1 GENERAL INTRODUCTION
By Syd Hoare

What follows is my translation of an article on Kenshiro Abe published in 1985 or thereabouts in a Japanese magazine. The un-named author appears to have been a Japanese writer/journalist and judoka who trained in one of the specialist high schools (Kosen) about the same time as Abe. Abe Kenshiro spent some time in the UK and there are still a few who can remember him there. This translation is for them. Abe was obviously excellent at Judo. But of interest to judoka, generally are some facts that emerge in this book concerning the rivalry between the Kodokan and the Butokukai (Busen) and how judo was in those days. There are a number of bitter remarks about the Kodokan, but these were voiced by the writer and are mostly in parenthesis " " . Where it says I (did this or that), the I refers to the writer. There are a number of remarks in brackets, which are my clarifications.

The twelve years or so from the beginning of the Showa period, 1926 to about 1940 was perhaps the peak of Japanese judo. This was when judo or kendo were compulsory subjects in middle school and judo thrived in ordinary high schools, specialist high schools, universities, in the armed forces and in machi (street) dojos. Technique and spirit reached the heights of development. One could say that present day judo is a pale shadow of the judo of that time.

Syd

2 EARLY LIFE

There are only a few in the Japanese judo world who remember the name Abe Kenshiro. But perhaps, there are still some in the UK who remember him from when he taught judo there. In Japan, by the 1950-60s, he was not included alongside past great judo men. Even when his name was occasionally mentioned by those who knew him, in most cases, he was portrayed as an eccentric character. In Japan, there is a popular saying, *"before Kimura Masahiko there was nobody; and after him there was nobody."* Kimura was at his peak around 1936 when he won several "All-Japan championships". The name Kimura became almost an adjective to describe someone of super-champion class. Those who knew Kimura did not think this was an exaggeration and many pamphlets and announcers described him in this manner. However, it was said that there was only one man who could throw Kimura *'all over the place'* and that was Kenshiro Abe.

Figure 1 Portrait of Abbe in his dojo when he was in the UK

So, what are the facts about this elusive character? The public records of him states that he was the fourth son of Abe Toshizo (or Rizo perhaps) of Tokushima prefecture, Myozai county, on the island of Shikoku. His village was situated among rice fields about 1.9km south from the Yoshinogawa river.

Figure 2 The river is 194 km long and has a watershed of 3,750 km2. It is the second longest river in Shikoku and is regarded as one of the three greatest rivers of Japan. Currently, tourists can enjoy rafting in the river (Wikipedia)

Figure 3 The Yoshino rises from Mount Kamegamori and flows to the east (Wikipedia)

Figure 4 The river eventually pours out into the Kii Channel (Wikipedia)

Figure 5 The 'Amagoi Falls' is a popular tourist attraction in Tokushima (Wikipedia)

Mountains were near and the area later became a national old folks retirement area. Nearby, there are still three houses carrying the family name of Abe. The family occupied a plot of just under 2 acres. The father and head of the house Toshizo, was headmaster of the local primary school. He married a local girl and between them, they had four sons and five daughters. The five girls were born first. The oldest son of the Abe household, Kiyoshi, trained as a secondary school teacher and taught at the local primary school. However, when his father died, he re-trained as a dentist in Osaka where he eventually worked and lived. Kenshiro obviously came from an educated family. At school, Kenshiro did not exactly dislike studying. But his most favorite time was when they did sumo. His physique was not anything special, but he was the best at sumo in his school and in the area.

A fateful move for Kenshiro was when he entered middle school (now the Kawashima High school) in 1927. As Judo was not practiced at his middle school, he joined the basketball group there. Then in his second year, an ex- police officer who held the rank 3rd Dan by the name of Nakamoto, set up a judo section in the school which Kenshiro gladly joined. Apart from sumo, judo and basketball, there is no record of him doing any other martial arts. However, during his time in the Japanese army, he would certainly have trained in jukendo (bayonet fighting).

Figure 6 Kawashima High School, now known as Kawashima Junior High School, as it stands currently (Wikipedia)

Nakamoto was a fine teacher and Kenshiro was inspired by him. Between the two of them, their energies combined. In the spring of his third middle school year, Kenshiro was graded to 1st Kyu. And then in the autumn of the same year, he won his 1st Dan. In his fourth year, he got his 2nd Dan and later in his fifth year, he was graded to 3rd Dan, aged 19. In 1925, there was probably no other instance in the whole country of a 19-year-old middle school student being graded 3rd Dan. In his promotion exam, Kenshiro beat all the other ten examinees. The man who came to grade them was Butokukai HQ 8th Dan (and Hanshi) Tabata Shotaro (later Kodokan 10th Dan). After the grading, Tabata strongly urged Kenshiro to join the Butokukai Specialist Martial Arts school (Busen) in Kyoto.

Figure 7 A wide shot of the Busen college (Wikipedia)

Figure 8 A membership pin from the Busen college

3 BUSEN COLLEGE

During this period, Abe formed the technical basis of his judo, which was ashi-barai, harai-tsurikomi ashi, uchimata, hane-goshi and tai-otoshi. Up to this point, Tokushima prefecture did not produce any top-class judoka. However, from his fourth year at middle school, nobody in the prefecture could stand up to him or his school team. As his graduation from middle school approached, his judo coach Nakamoto as well as others urged him to apply to the Butokukai Specialist Martial Arts College. As it happened, one student from his school by the name of Aoyama, who was a year ahead of him, had already entered Busen, which created a useful connection. There were other specialist martial arts colleges in the east of Japan such as the Tokyo Koshiko (probably Kano's Koto Shihan Gakko is meant here), the Tokyo Koshi Taiiku-ka (Tokyo Special Physical Education Course) and the Kokushikan College, all for middle school graduates who wanted to become college judo/kendo teachers or police instructors. However, it was the Butokukai Specialist College that attracted the best.

When you are engaged in the right natural posture, advance your left foot. Your opponent will retreat on his right foot.

Then, by the application of the *tsurikomi* movement with both hands, break his balance towards his left front corner.

When his balance has been broken, advance your left foot close to his right foot

Stretch out your right leg, and with the sole of your right foot sweep the ankle or the bottom of the shin of his left leg backwards and inwards, i. e., away from you.

At the same time twist your upper body to the right and strongly pull your right hand holding his left lapel towards your right armpit.

Your left hand holding his right sleeve assists this movement by pushing upwards to your right.

Your opponent falls towards his left side in a large circle.

Figure 9 Technical details of Harai tsurikomi ashi

13

Figure 10 Demonstration of tai-otoshi

Each year, the Kokushikan signed up twenty judo and twenty kendo students, although as many as 150 students applied to enter either course. Abe applied to the Kokushikan which had an earlier entrance exam than the rest. This was on the advice of some other Tokushima prefecture students who had previously taken the entrance exam. The judo/kendo course had an entry competition. Abe qualified for this by easily beating three other would-be entrants.

Figure 11 The Kokushinkan school in the Shoin shrine located in Setagaya, 1917 (Kokushikan)

Figure 12 The university as it stands today, at Setagaya, Tokyo (Wikipedia)

Figure 13 The university was originally founded by Tokujiro Shibata in 1917 (Wikipedia)

Attending this competition was Kudo Kazuzo of the Tokyo Koshi college and the Kodokan. After the judo matches, Kudo called Abe over and said, *"I take it that you will enter the Kokushikan if you are accepted!"*. Kudo was apparently anxious to sign him up. However, Abe replied, *"I will talk it over with my parents."* Normally a student could have given an ambiguous reply. But 19-year-old Abe went on further without hesitation by stating, *"After this exam I will try for Busen and if they accept me that is where I will enter."* Kudo's expression hardened and he said nothing.

Figure 14 Kudo Kazuzo was a direct student of Jigoro Kano and authored several books on Judo (Goodreads)

Soon after in the Busen entrance competition, Abe won two matches and drew the third. This made him second after an individual named Azuma, who had quit the Kokushikan after one year. Having been accepted for Busen, the next problem to face was how Abe was to live in Kyoto. There were several schools (juku) which also provided accommodation for the students including the Isogai-juku. But there was no juku which catered for students from Shikoku. Despite this, Abe was not deterred. Once, Coach Nakamoto said of Abe that he was indifferent to his personal appearance and that he was like an oak branch which once bent, never returns to its original position.

Abe then begged his 56-year-old mother to accompany him to Kyoto. She answered, *"This will be my last duty to my child. I will serve you with our family's special fried dragon-flies and I will go to Kyoto."* She then sold off half the land, rented out part of the remainder for cultivation and found a house to rent near Shika-ga-tani in Kyoto. Just before this, Abe's older sister gave up her job as dental assistant to her older brother in Osaka and came to live with them in Kyoto. Busen was housed in a two-floor reinforced concrete building behind the wooden Butokuden (Military Virtues Palace) in the Heian Shrine precinct. The judo section had its own 250 mat dojo for sole use. But occasionally, it used the 400 mat great dojo in the Butokuden.

At the usual welcome party for new students, Abe was perplexed. All were expected to drink a lot of alcohol. But Abe refused, saying that he did not drink. Eventually, all were asked to sing a song. Those students who knew Abe well knew that he was so concentrated on his judo that he was hardly able to do anything else. Eventually, Abe's turn came around. He announced that since he could not do anything, he would recite one poem (a short waka) from the recollections of Kumazawa Banzan, a reforming samurai of the 17th century. With a fairly resonant voice, he recited it and the noise around him soon died down. *"Though my anxieties now pile up, I will test myself to the very limits of my body"*. The second part of the poem faithfully reflects the life of Abe at the Busen and indeed for the rest of his life thereafter.

At Busen, the daily programs were literature in the morning, namely Japanese, classical Chinese, physiology, and hygiene. From 1.30 - 3pm there was technical training led by the Busen teachers. And from 3 - 4.30pm, there was free practice. At the coldest and hottest times of the year, there were special hot and cold training periods (kangeiko and doyogeiko) from 6am – 7.30am.

Figure 15 Judokas engaging in a 30-day winter training (kangeiko) at the Kodokan. The training would have been similar, or more intense at the Busen college.

The judo teachers included Isogai, Tabata and Kurihara. Isogai was quite old and did not do randori with the students. But the other teachers did, especially Kurihara, who was known as Devil Kurihara. All three later became Kodokan 10th Dans. Three years previously in 1929, Kurihara won the first of the prestigious Tenran Shiai, which was held in front of the Emperor, by beating Ushijima in the finals. When Abe practiced with Kurihara, he always lost no matter how hard he tried. Kurihara handled him easily. In particular, he would catch and pull one of Abe's arms and quickly get a joint lock on it. Abe had no means to stop it (this was probably a standing armlock).

Figure 16 Tamio Kurihara (left) takes on Tatsukuma Ushijima with Yoshitsugu Yamashita watching over. This was at the final of Shōwa Tenran Jiai in 1929 (Wikipedia)

Figure 17 Tamio Kurihara was a graduate of the Busen college and later served as an instructor in many places. Towards the end of his life in October of 1965, he received the Shiju Houshou, Purple Ribbon Medal (Judo channel)

Figure 18 Tatsukuma Ushijima, also known as 'Devil Ushijima', is well known for being the teacher of the great Masahiko Kimura (Wikipedia)

Figure 19 Shotaro Tabata joined the Kodokan in the early 1900s and later became an instructor at the Busen college. He was associated with Hajime Isogai. Tabata was awarded his 10th Dan in 1948 (Judo channel)

Figure 20 Isogai was considered to be an expert in ne-waza. He was well known for his feud with Jujutsu practitioner, Mataemon Tanabe. He later became an instructor at the Kodokan and Busen college. In 1923, he was the 2nd person to be awarded a 10th Dan rank (judomododeusar)

Figure 21 : The winners of Shōwa Tenran Jiai in 1929. From left to right: Hisao Kihara, Tamio Kurihara, Moriji Mochida and Yokoyama (Wikipedia)

Figure 22 Front gate leading into the Busen (McCall, George)

It goes without saying that at Busen, the first-year students were roughly tossed about (bullied/hazed) by all the other students. Abe often trained with Hirata, the captain of the first year. At first, Abe got thrown around by him. But soon later, he caught up with him.

Figure 23 Hirata, after winning the Tenran Jiai in 1934 (McCall, George)

In the autumn of his first year at Busen (1932), Abe was graded to 4th Dan. The following year, Abe's sister Toyoko got interested in the Naginata (halberd) and joined the Busen classes in that martial art under sensei Nishigaki Kin. Often when she had finished her training, she would come and watch her brother train. Eventually, she wrote a book on the naginata and taught it twice a week. Toyoko heard of a five-room house up for rental from a Kyoto University medical professor. It was near the Heian Shrine and the Butokuden. As a result, together with her brother and mother, they moved into the house. There were two other empty rooms which she rented out to Busen students, probably from the island of Shikoku.

Figure 24 Abe Toyoko sharing her views on Naginata with Ellis Amdur and Kini Collins in the 1980s (Collins, Kini)

Figure 25 Abe Toyoko practicing Tendo-ryu nitojutsu (Collins, Kini)

Figure 26 The Heian Shrine, as it stands today at Sakyo-ku, Kyoto (Wikipedia)

The judo free-fighting session at the Butokuden consisted of ten to fifteen randori without a rest. Abe nearly always did the most, he always carried on throwing. And in turn, he was thrown to the point where he staggered around from exhaustion, facing down on the mat and barely able to rise. There were others who suffered the same fate. Whereupon the teaching assistants and the senior students would shout out, *"You haven't done enough, get up!"* and kick them up on to their feet. The dojo often presented a harrowing sight. Immediately after the Manchurian Incident (1931) when Japan annexed Manchuria, there was little employment to be had in Japan. Getting a job based on PE qualifications, which was what the Busen students were hoping for, required the degree of severity as described above or so the teachers seemed to believe.

Figure 27 Japanese troops gathering outside Mukden, Manchuria, September 1931 (Swift, John)

Every Saturday afternoon, training competitions were held in the Busen. Toyoko often went to watch. According to her, she never saw her brother being beaten in these training competitions. The stronger judoka was often given five-man line ups with each bout lasting five minutes. When he took on his five-man line-up, Abe fought two 2nd Dans, two 3rd Dans and one 4th Dan. It only took him about two minutes to finish them off. When he did that, Isogai would cry out, *"Have you finished already!"* and give him another line-up.

There were even times when Isogai or Tabata would give him a 3rd five-man line-up. In the autumn of his second year in Busen, Abe was promoted to 5th Dan. The teaching staff at Busen were not in the habit of praising students including Abe. Their expression of feelings towards their students were only expressed in the amount of training they made them do. On Saturday evenings, most Busen students would go out for a drink. Some of them would visit the licensed quarters of Kyoto, looking for women. Kenshiro Abe however never drank or smoked and did not like the company of his contemporaries that much. He never thought to buy sex, make money, or expose his inner self.

When he returned home after training, he would read what his seniors described as 'difficult books' such as philosophy. In his third or fourth year, he read all of Tanabe Hajime's 'Outline of Philosophy' in the Iwanami series. He also crept secretly into lectures given by Tanabe Hajime at the Kyoto Imperial University. In later years, Abe smiled wryly and said, *"I don't think I understood them that much."* Certainly, no one else from Busen did.

Figure 28 Hajime Tanabe was a philosopher from the Kyoto University. He was awarded the Order of Cultural Merit in 1950 for his contributions towards Japanese literature and philosophy (Wikipedia)

One thing that Abe often did on returning home was to visit a nursery playground next to Nanzenji temple, usually accompanied by his sister. The playground was lit by a few small lanterns. But in winter, it was quite dark. Clad in shorts, Abe would rope-skip in periods from 5 minutes up to 20 minutes with Toyoko calling out the times upon which he would briefly rest before continuing. Mixed in was other types of skipping, such as double skips and rear skipping. Abe later explained that this type of training made his footwork faster. He went onto explain the importance of footwork for sports, especially judo. Abe recommended this to his contemporaries and junior students.

Figure 29 The Nanzenji temple, located at the base of Higashiyama mountains, is one of the most important Zen temples in all of Japan (Wikipedia)

I have never heard of any judo man recommending rope-skipping daily as a form of training for judo. He may have gotten the idea from boxing training. Abe's okuri-ashi-harai, tsubame-gaeshi and his harai-tsurikomi-ashi which he did from a very upright posture were unlike any others in Japan for speed and sharpness. On moonlit nights, he ventured out to the nursery playground and went at his training even harder. His skipping made him run with sweat even in winter.

At other times, he went to the part of the playground that had swings with sand underneath and practiced somersaults with or without assistance. When it was too wet, he laid cushions on his veranda and practiced upstarts, flicking back on to one's feet from a back-lying position. In addition to this, he worked out with chest expanders. Around this time, he fought several top-class judokas and in one instance, he successfully used centripetal force (kyushindo) to throw a much heavier opponent. Perhaps this was the start of his judo philosophy of kyushindo.

Abe was lucky in one aspect, and that was the care he received from his sister Toyoko. Along with cooking for him, she treated his injuries and washed his judogi. When the judogi was washed and dried, she folded it and placed it in the Tokonoma (recess space) in the room. When questioned about this, she would say for a judoman. The judogi is like a samurai's armour and it is appropriate to place the gi there. He was also the object of a physiological research (The Biology of Fatigue) by Professor Kyugo Sasagawa, a Kyoto University medical professor. This lasted for a few years. During the summer holidays, the majority of Busen students returned to their hometowns. During this holiday, it was usual for the All-Japan Specialist High Schools (Kosen) to hold their championships in the Butoku-den. Abe attended these events and learnt a lot about Kosen-judo.

Since the Kosen competitors could do as much groundwork as they liked and usually chose nothing but groundwork, it was not necessary to have the wide fifty mat contest area as with Kodokan judo. The contest format was to have fifteen competitors in each team, where the winner stays on. It was not unusual to see a competitor fight for 30 or even 40 minutes. This was similar to medieval jujitsu groundwork. From the start, Busen judo was on par with Kodokan judo; both aimed at a tachi-waza and ne-waza mix to a ratio of 80%-20%. The Kyoto based No.3 Specialist High School often held Kosen style matches with Busen and they were well matched.

At the time, there was no recorded instance of the Tokyo Keishicho (police) with its direct connection with either the Kodokan, or Tokyo based Waseda University, at its zenith beating a first class Kosen high school (this probably meant under Kosen judo rules). From quite early, in 1932, Abe became the captain (Taisho) of the 22 new Busen first year students. Among them were many strong students. Abe often participated in the group practice (godokeiko) between Busen, Kyoto No.3 Specialist High School, and the Doshisha University attached commercial high school.

Doshisha won the national upper middle school championships sponsored by the Mainichi newspaper and Kyoto University. And eventually in 1937, it won the national high-school championships. Abe often said that we (Busen?) were not a problem for them. It was rare for a judoman to say that. I once asked Fumio Hosotani (a later Busen teacher), if Abe was not so strong on the ground. In contrary, Hosotani replied, *"No, he was very strong at groundwork and supple."* Hosotani even acted as a groundwork advisor to the Japanese 1964 Olympic team. Isao Okano once cited Hosotani as an influence on his style of judo.

Figure 30 The front gate leading into Doshisha University, photographed between 1912-1926 (Wikipedia)

When Hosotani's team won the 1934 All-Japan middle school championships, it met with the Chinzai middle school, which was captained by Kimura Masahiko and beat them. Kimura was already an exceptional 4th Dan Middle school student. When the Kodokan specialists heard about him, they travelled to Kumomoto to observe and train with him. However, they were mercilessly dealt with. Kimura did eventually end up fighting for the Tokyo based Takushoku University.

These middle school championships consisted of teams of six and were fought under Kosen rules in which groundwork was at the center. As we have seen above, Abe was a bit of a philosopher. During his 3rd year at Busen, he wrote a critique of Takagi Naoyuki's 'Scientific Study of Judo' (Biological Studies No. 6), which is still worth reading. In it, Takagi writes that those who mainly do standing judo, praise throwing principles to the skies. And those who do mainly groundwork, similarly, praise its principles. But the scope of judo he wrote, is very wide and contains special principles and urges judoka to practice both standing and groundwork. Abe presumably agreed with this since he was mainly a tachi-waza man.

It seems that both Kimura and Abe were both very competent on the ground and in standing, and that they could win whatever the rules. Around this time, Kodokan judo (east Japan) was characterized as being throwing judo and Kansai (west Japan) judo, as being groundwork judo. The Kodokan changed the rules in 1925 to restrict the growth of groundwork-only contest. This was done by the Kodokan to stop Kosen judo winning. Kosen judo lost its power following the war defeat. But before the war, it was very influential and opposed Kodokan judo. (see my *A History of Judo* for a different interpretation - Syd Hoare) There is no record of Kimura reading Abe's critique or being influenced by it. But without doubt, it was Kimura who perfected judo with his equal emphasis on both types of judo at a critical time following the 1925 Kodokan contest rule changes which limited groundwork opportunities.

Figure 31 Portrait of Masahiko Kimura (Lifejudo)

4 JUDO PROGRESSION

In 1936, Abe graduated from Busen but stayed on as an assistant instructor. Other strong Busen graduates such as Ogawa and Ito Tokuhara also stayed on. Ito was much taller and heavier than Abe, who studied how to beat him. He was a perfect object of research for Abe. However, Ito was a tad slower than Abe who could predict his moves. Ito respected Abe and often asked for his advice on technique. In 1937, Matsumoto Yasuichi graduated from the Fukuoka Myozen Middle School and entered Busen. He was 187cm tall and weighed 79kg. Later, he went on to win the All-Japan Championships in 1948. At the age of 38, he participated in a lot of competitions up to the 1st World Championships of 1956 where he just failed to represent Japan in the selection contests. He lost to Yoshimatsu in the semi-final.

Matsumoto was a fierce fighter and memorable were his matches against Kimura, whom he fought four times. Perhaps, his most legendary match against Kimura was in Fukuoka in 1948 in the final of the Shinsei Judo Taikai. The match was extended seven times and lasted about fifty minutes. Toward the end of the match, Matsumoto's arm was broken by Kimura's Ude-garami and both men fell off the raised contest area. Matsumoto climbed back up with his arm hanging uselessly at his side and advanced again on Kimura crying out loudly *"Sa koi!"* (come on then!). Confusion reigned among the judges, but the referee stopped the match and gave the match to Kimura, *"Itami-wake!"*.

Figure 32 Yasuichi Matsumoto was noted for winning the All-Japan championships in 1948. He later became an All-Japan Judo Federation Olympic Coach in the early 1970's (Wikipedia)

When Matsumoto first entered Busen, he weighed 79kg and Abe only came up to his shoulder. When they first fought, Abe unleashed a barrage of attacks and handled him easily. The highest ranked captain of Busen was Hirose who weighed 92kg at a height of 164cm. In the 1950s, Hirose often fought in the All-Japan Championships. Abe handled him as easily as he did with Matsumoto who thought that Abe had something magical in his body. He could beat them all. Matsumoto, Hosotani, contemporaries, seniors and juniors all regarded Abe as someone unique. Not only did he play with them in training, but he taught them all the techniques and principles of judo.

According to Abe, all the rigid bones in the body are linked by joints. Which means that the bones can only move in complicated circles. To throw someone, the thrower has to consider how to use this circular movement effectively. When teaching, Abe would often call out somebody as a partner and analyze ways in which this could be done. This was based not only on his training experience but on his understanding of the principles involved; particularly Kyushindo (centripetal force) and Banbutsu ruten (all things are set in motion and flow). Matsumoto and others wondered if Abe's methods were not based on the application of physics and dynamics to judo. Abe apparently wrote an article for the Busen Alumni magazine entitled *'Osotogari Ron: An Essay on Osotogari.'*

Figure 33 The logo for 'kyushindo' which Abbe used later in his life when teaching

If any of his Busen students lost in an unsightly way, Abe would get angry and complain. He was always concerned that his students should grow. His fine detailed instruction was part of this. Abe's best major competitions results occurred during the period 1934-36. The first in 1934 was the Internal-External Red & White Team Championships (Naigai-chi Taiko Judo Kohaku Shiai Taikai). This event was under the auspices of the Colonization Ministry and consisted of mainland Japan (naichi) against external Japan (gaichi) including Korea and Manchuria etc.

Abe 5th Dan, participated in this for the internal team and there is a record of him beating a Kimura Minoru 4th Dan and one other 4th Dan called Kadowaki of the Dairen Police in China. (From my research, there was a judoka named Seiichiro Kadowaki. He was born in 1886 and trained directly under Jigoro Kano. He received his 6th Dan in 1932 and acted as an instructor to the Tokyo Metropolian Police Department.

It is unlikely that he is the same Kadowaki mentioned here – Abdul Rashid)

Kimura is a common surname in Japan and the rest of the names mentioned is not the same as that of the great Masahiko Kimura. Abe is also a common Japanese surname and several Abe's can be found in the contest records. The internal group won this event. However, I was still determined to chase up the story of how Abe easily beat the great Kimura. I had several interviews with those who had close connection with Kimura, such as Yamaguchi and Ushijima, who was Kimura's teacher.

The second competition in 1935 seems to have been an incredibly special one and was between five of the top 5th Dans in Japan. I checked what records were available about this time and discovered one small reference in an Asahi Newspaper of 1936. It mentioned about a 'winner-stays-on' match held the year before, in May 1935, between five top fifth Dans in the dojo within the Imperial Palace grounds. A clue to possible imperial presence was the fact that after the individual bouts, Ushijima then took on all the 5th Dans in a line-up. It seems to have been quite a formal set-up. The top 5th Dans were Kimura of Takudai, Osawa Yoshimi of the police, Murata from Hokkaido, Sato of the Palace police and Abe of Busen. I also interviewed those who had witnessed the competition. According to one account, when Abe closed with Kimura, it was done fairly gently. This reinforces the view that a member of the Imperial family was present and that they may have been expected to put on a good show.

Figure 34 1934 Tenran Jiai with Emperor Hirohito overseeing (Chen, Peter)

Figure 35 View of a bridge outside the Imperial Palace, 1923

Figure 36 At the time of this publication, Yoshimi Osawa is one of 3 living 10th Dans, along with Ichiro Abe and Toshiro Daigo (Wikipedia)

Figure 37 A recent photo of Yoshimi Osawa, Toshiro Daigo and Ichiro Abe taken in 2020 (Bigot, Patrick)

Figure 38 Kimura with a gift from the emperor after winning the Tenran Jiai in 1940
(Wikipedia)

Abe scored a waza-ari in the opening seconds of the match with harai-tsurikomi-ashi. Then as Kimura rose to his feet, Abe swept him down again on to his head with ashi-barai. Abe then went on to win all his remaining bouts very quickly. At that time, Abe was arguably the strongest judoman in Japan. This was the culminating point of his judo career. The third competition was when he beat three 5th Dans in a row. It took place on April 30th, 1936, on the first Zen-Nippon Tozai Taiko Shiai (All-Japan East versus West Team Championships). This was held in Fukuoka in Kyushu. Kimura did not participate in this competition.

The match was fought with the best thirty-two men from each region in a 'winner stays on' basis. The first man out the senpo (spearhead) would be good for obvious reasons. But from him to the last and strongest man would be the captain (Taisho). The teams would be arranged in roughly ascending grade order. Abe came out to fight early on for the West team (9th from the Senpo). Judo thrived in the East, meaning the Tokyo area and further north. And in the West, it thrived in Kyoto, Kyushu, Shikoku, Osaka, and Kobe. So, it was understandable that the first East-West Tournament (Tozai Taiko Taikai) should be held in Fukuoka.

The land mass of the west of Japan was quite a bit smaller than the eastern section. So, Manchuria, Korea (at the time part of the Japanese empire) and Taiwan were included in the Western camp as well. Qualification for either team depended on place of residence and 32 of the best competitors were selected to represent each team. The Fukuoka Daily Newspaper carried quite a lot of eye-catching stories on its front page about the competition from just over a month before the match.

The captain of the East team was a 39-year-old 7th Dan by the name of Kinnosuke Sato. The captain of the West team was a 46-year-old 7th Dan, Uto Torao. Both captains and vice-captains were previous winners of the All-Japan Championships.

Figure 39 Kinnosuke Sato (left) up against Tatsukuma Ushijima in 1929 (Wikipedia)

Figure 40 Kinnosuke Sato, 9th Dan, idolized Kyuzo Mifune whom he trained under. Later in his life, he received a teaching license from the Busen college and was the vice chairman of the Tokyo Judo Federation. (Wikipedia)

Figure 41 Tarao Uto was also known as the 'Father of Kumamoto Modern Sports' due to his contributions as a sports coach. He entered the Kodokan in 1913 at the age of 22 and eventually worked his way up to 9th Dan. In 1937, he was invited to the US by the American Judo Federation for physical education research. (Wikipedia)

Although both men were veterans, I observed that they were still training hard around 1947. These champions knew each other's judo well. So, it seemed that the match would probably be decided by two or three of the younger 6th Dans or by some of the larger group of 5th Dans which numbered about 24 judokas. The core of the East team consisted of graduates of the Tokyo Koto Shihan Gakko, the Kodokan, and students from private and government universities. The Western team centered on graduates of the Butokukai Senmon Gakko. There were also some students still studying and judo people from Kyushu. It was basically a Kodokan versus Butokukai match.

The Tokyo Koto Shihan Gakko (Tokyo Teachers Training College, Higher Normal School) was headed by Kano Jigoro for many years and obviously had direct links to the Kodokan. Busen was part of the Butokukai Foundation, which was staffed by Hajime Isogai and Shuichi Nagaoka, who were students sent there by Kano in the beginning. Eventually, Busen influence matured and came to rival the Koto Shihan Gakko and/or the Kodokan. The two teams were well balanced, and the matches were fought for only one Ippon and not for Yuseigachi (superiority) wins. It was not easy to make even one win. So, winning one bout then staying on to take on the next person and getting a draw was considered outstanding. In the lead up to the match, the local newspaper did several profiles of the contestants.

Figure 42 The Shihan Gakko, pictured above, was established in 1872 and acted as a training institute for teachers. It went through several name changes, from Shihan Gakko to the Tokyo Koto Shihan Gakko (Yasuoki, Noguchi)

Figure 43 Kendo training in the Koto Shihan Gakko, 1917 (McCall, George)

Figure 44 Professor Jigoro Kano, middle, with the track and field team. He was the headmastership of the Tokyo Koto Shihan Gakko for 23 years (Wikipedia)

Figure 45 Succeeding the Tokyo Koto Shihan Gakko, the Hiroshima Higher Normal School was the 2nd training institute established in Japan in 1902. Sadly, it was destroyed by the atomic bomb in 1945. (Wikipedia)

Figure 46 Shuichi Nagaoka initially trained in Kito-Ryu Jujutsu under Noda Kensaburo before joining the Kodokan. He was well known for his sutemi waza and feud with Mataemon Tanabe. He was one of 3 individuals to be promoted to 10th Dan by Jigoro Kano (Samurai arts)

Kenshiro Abe is mentioned here and there among them. His reputation was stronger in the Kyoto area than anywhere else. A photo of Abe shows him as a round-faced, close-cropped youth with a serious expression. The average height and weight of the West team competitors was 168cm and 79kg. Compare this to the average height and weight of the All-Japan entrants in 1986 which was 180cm and 106kg. The tickets for the championships quickly sold out. The match was reported on all over Kyushu and in the cities of Kyushu, people gathered around the notice boards where the results were written up.

On the day of the championships, the officials including Jigoro Kano and the competitors, gathered in lines to listen to the various speeches of welcome and to exchange greetings. When their names were being read out, Abe Kenshiro ran forward from his line, bowed, and then ran back. It was not clear what he did exactly. The other players watched this wondered what he was up to. Etiquette in those days was strictly observed. I still remember the strong impression I received from this incident. This was perhaps an early indication of his eccentricity.

Figure 47 Jigoro Kano in Berlin, 1936 (Wikipedia)

At 1200hrs the event began. The referees were headed by Mifune Kyuzo, who was then an 8th Dan and a Kodokan man.

Figure 48 Kyuzo Mifune, 10th Dan, is considered to be one of the greatest Judo technicians (Alchetron)

The matches were 20 minutes for the captains, 15 minutes for the vice-captains and 8 minutes for the rest. The first match was won by the East 5th Dan Senpo (spearhead) with Ushiro-goshi. Two drawn matches followed. Then Ajioka of the East team won with Osotogari. Then the next four matches were drawn. After which, Abe Kenshiro came on to the mat. At this point, the East team was leading by two matches. Abe then disposed of three 5th Dans in a row and lost his fourth match on the ground. Abe's first win was with Osoto-makikomi, then Osoto-gaeshi and then Osoto-makikomi again. The tournament continued with a lot of drawn matches (23 in total!) and a sprinkling of wins on either side. But eventually, the West team won 7 matches to 6. It was Kenshiro Abe and his three wins which had decided the match. In one of those matches, both contestants fell off the one-meter-high contest area. Abe's left leg was injured, but this did not stop him.

There was one more All-Japan Competition which Abe participated in when he was 37 years old, in 1950. One wonders what he was thinking of. His dislocated shoulder left his right arm virtually useless, and his loss of muscle could be plainly seen. He had also become a heavy smoker in the army but could not be dissuaded from competing. His shaven head shone as he climbed up on to the mat. In his first match, he met Mori of Yamaguchi prefecture who he beat with Yoko-shiho-gatame, a rare groundwork win for him. In round two, he came up against the famous Ishikawa who he beat with Abise-taoshi. However, the record here must be wrong because Ishikawa won this competition by defeating Hirose in the final.

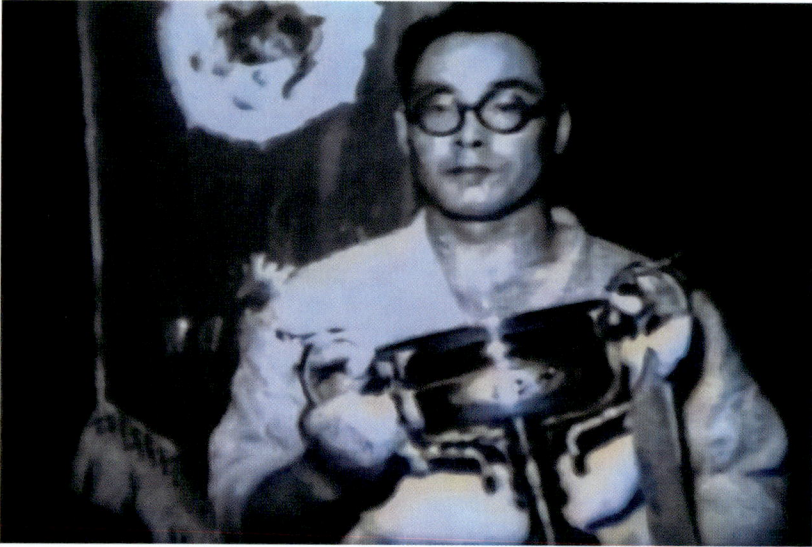

Figure 49 Takahiko Ishikawa was the All-Japan Judo Champion in 1949 and 1950. He was well known for his dedication as a Judo instructor. He co-authored the famous 'Judo Training Methods' book with the famed Donn Draeger (Sharp, Harold)

Figure 50 Iwao Hirose, Kodokan 9th Dan, was a student of both the Busen college and later the Kodokan. He later instructed in various institutions such as the Kyoto Prefectural University of Medicine, Osaka Imperial University and Osaka Police Department. He even served as a referee in the 1964 Olympics. (Wikipedia)

At the time, I was a third-year student at the Fukui Commercial High School and trained in judo there. I was a great fan of Kimura but at the same time had great respect for Abe. Some 17 years later, I talked with Toshio Yamaguchi who at 100kg, was in the top rank of Japanese judo. We eventually got on to the subject of Abe. Yamaguchi and Kimura both turned pro-wrestlers at the same time. Yamaguchi once fought a draw with Kimura in a match between Tokyo Federation students versus the Manchurian army team. I asked Yamaguchi who was the strongest judo-man of that time, and he replied, *"Abe, he was fantastic."* He went on to relate that the day before the first East-West tournament, there was a practice session for all. Abe handled them all during the practice. If Abe had not injured himself in the actual tournament, he might have beaten five or six in a row.

JUDO STARS SIGN — Masayuki Kimura (seated) and Toshio
Yamaguchi (standing), two of Japan's greatest judo wrestlers,
yesterday signed with Promoter Al Karasick to appear on his
pro mat cards at the Civic auditorium. Kimura and Yamaguchi
will be featured on this Sunday night's card. (Jack Matsumoto
photo.)

Figure 51 Toshio Yamaguchi (middle) along with Masahiko Kimura in Hawaii during their
pro-wrestling days (Aikido sangenkai)

In 1935, Kimura finished his studies at the Chinzai middle school and entered Takushoku (Takudai) University's preparatory course in Tokyo, where Ushijima was the chief sensei and Shihan. Kimura lodged in Ushijima's dormitory and trained 7-8 hours per day. Kimura was famous for his intensive training and dedication towards judo. In that same year, Kimura won the All-Japan University Kosen Students championships and in the following year, he was captain of the Takudai team which won the national Kosen championships. This was the Kanto (East) area's one and only medal. Kimura put a lot of effort into groundwork, among other things. Eventually, he developed an ude-garami that all his opponent feared. There were several recorded instances of Kimura breaking arms. I once met an ude-garami expert in the Kodokan who showed me a lot of ude-garami variations and entries.

Figure 52 Kimura himself demonstrating a standup version of the Gyaku Ude Garami
(Danaher, John)

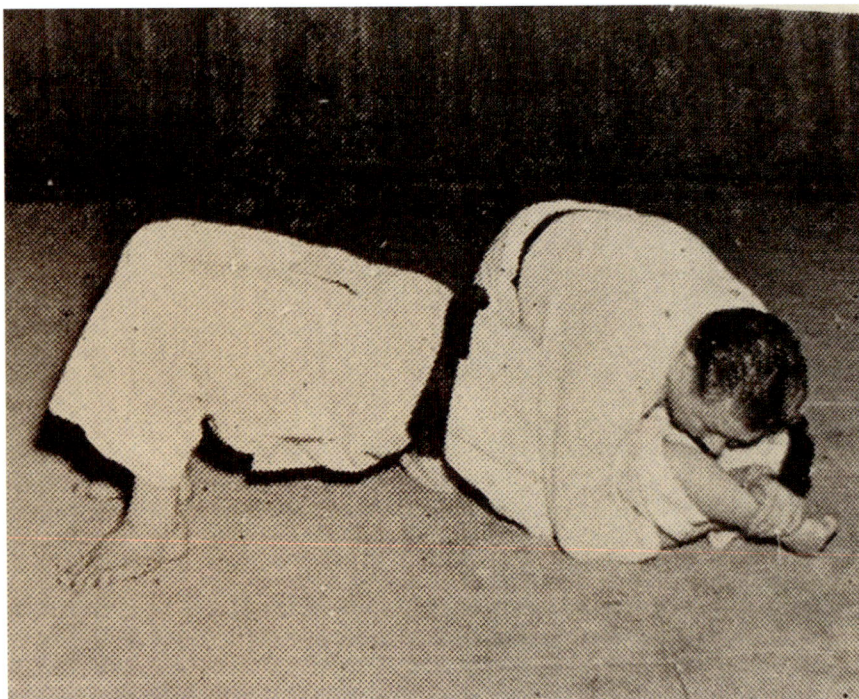

Figure 53 An instructor from the Kodokan demonstrating an Ude Garami from side control

5 IMPERIAL ARMY

In June of 1937, Abe enlisted for active service with the Tokushima 43rd Infantry Regiment. This was partly to do with the fact that Abe had finished his studies at Busen and that his exemption from military service had run out. In July 1937, the so called Lugou Bridge Incident occurred on the outskirts of Beijing between Japanese and Chinese troops. This minor incident was used by the Japanese to rush reinforcements to Hopei province, which eventually led to a war between China and Japan. Patriotic duty required young Japanese men to enlist rather than waiting to be called up.

Figure 54 Infantry Regiment in the 1920s

Figure 55 The Marco Polo (Lugou) Bridge Incident was a conflict between the Republic of China's National Revolutionary Army and the Imperial Japanese Army. It is widely considered to have been the start of the Second Sino-Japanese War. Here, the bridge is photographed around 1937 (Seniram)

Figure 56 Chinese sentry at the Lugou Bridge. The dispute started after a Japanese soldier went AWOL during a training exercise in Wanping. There were speculations that the Chinese troops may have captured him. After failed negotiations, the Japanese proceeded to invade Wanping (Chen, Peter)

Figure 57 The bridge as it stands currently (Wikipedia)

Abe had several judo injuries including a dislocated shoulder which an over excited student inflicted on him when he was bowing. It continued to trouble him for many years after. If he had mentioned this during his enlistment examination, he might have been rejected for service or exempted for longer. But Abe saw his duty clearly. He was soon sent to a wilderness in Manchuria (Manchukuo) in north-east China which was controlled by the Japanese Kwantung army. This was an infantry group based in Port Arthur (Ryojun in Japanese) with an HQ in Hsinking. The army's role was to guard and control the strategic area East of the Pass. This army had a ferocious reputation. But towards the end of the war, it was severely mauled by soviet mechanized forces. The army became very independent of Tokyo control and dictated the course of the war in China.

Figure 58 The Kwantung Army was an army group of the Imperial Japanese Army from 1919 to 1945.Picture above shows their headquarters located in Hsinking, Manchukuo (Manchuria), 1935 (Wikipedia)

It was also known as a hotbed of the Kodo-ha (Imperial faction). Abe was stationed there for four very turbulent years 1937-41. Almost nothing is known about his time in Manchuria, and one cannot help wondering how seriously this affected his later life and decisions. It seems he never wore a judo suit during the whole time he was there as a probationary officer. And neither did he do anything in the army that related to judo. (It seems that Kodokan judo made little inroad into the Japanese army which is curious when you think how strong judo was in the navy – Syd Hoare).

During his ten years of judo, Abe had rarely taken more than three days off from training. And consequently, he had built up a typical judo physique which inevitably declined during his time in the army. In 1941, he was promoted to second lieutenant and simultaneously discharged from military service before returning to Japan. He was then twenty-eight years old and had lost a lot of hair. On arriving back in Japan, he first went to his mother and older sister's place in east Teno-cho in Kyoto where his mother who was 65 began preparing for his return, cooking the traditional rice and red beans.

He spoke briefly to them, then picked up his gi and headed for the Busen. In the assistants' room, he greeted everybody, changed into his kit and went to the dojo where he began practicing breakfalls for the first time in four years. Isogai who was unaware of his arrival, heard him in the dojo and came running out and hugged him. His eyes moistened as he said, *"Ah Abe, you've returned. That's good."* Isogai who had never showed any emotion regarding Abe showed it for the first time. Like a fish released into water, Abe began training again. Remaining in the dojo were Matsumoto and Hosotani, who had entered Busen after their military service.

Ten days later, Matsumoto practiced with Abe. *"You are still strong but compared with when I first joined Busen, you have lost a bit of speed,"* he said. Hosotani also had a go with Abe on the ground and simply commented that Abe was breathing hard. Abe gradually increased the amount of training and after two months, he could take on three people in a row without losing his breath. His judo sense also returned to him. Soon after that, he got married. His wife was seven years younger than him and between them, they had three daughters. Unfortunately, the Greater East Asian War broke out and for a second time it looked like he would be stopped from doing judo. His former Lt. Col in the Kwantung army hearing that he had returned from Manchuria, called him from Kyoto and re-enlisted him in the army. *"Your discharge was a nonsense,"* he said, *"You should be the captain."* Abe became attached to the Tokushima Regiment again. Perhaps part of the reason for this was that he was a frequent Go playing partner of his colonel in Manchuria. Abe began regularly commuting from Kyoto to the Regiment's base in Tokushima.

It should be born in mind that the professional soldiers of the time, regardless of their intelligence, could virtually abuse anyone they wished. Life in the Japanese army was pretty brutal, and beatings were commonplace. Isogai was deeply disappointed with this turn of events. Someone who knew him in his time as a soldier said that Abe never talked about his judo successes. Abe used to cycle from his Kyoto home to the Regiment's office. The war situation got worse for Japan and the Tokushima Reserve Regiment was converted to an Assault Regiment. Abe was soon promoted to Daitaicho or Battalion Commander. This was a conscripted regiment staffed by Koreans who did not speak a word of Japanese.

(As already noted, almost nothing is known about Abe's four years in Kwantung 1937-41. Similarly, little is known about military record during the Pacific war 1941-45. Did he remain in Tokushima training new conscripts or did he go into active service in the Pacific, or did he return to Kwantung in China? - Syd Hoare)

As the Americans moved closer to a mainland attack, the Japanese constantly debated whether they would have to fight them on the beaches or retreat to the mountains. But their strategies frequently changed. They could not make up their minds. Eventually, the Americans dropped two nuclear bombs on Japan and the war came to an end.

Figure 59 Bombings of Hiroshima and Nagasaki (Wikipedia)

6 JAPAN'S WAR DEFEAT

After the 1941-45 war defeat, the Butokukai (Martial Virtues Society) and Busen were abolished. The Kodokan regained its monopoly of promotion and in Abe's words, *"over-issued Dan grades for large sums of money. The head of the Kodokan who had never worn a judogi in his life gave out grades to politicians who had also never worn judogis. This was to curry favor with the politicians"*. The Dan grade system was originally devised by Jigoro Kano and was an ingenious means of promoting judo. At the time however both the Kodokan and the Butokukai issued Dan grades. The Butokukai only had three ranks to start with: Renshi, Kyoshi & Hanshi. But it later copied the successful Kodokan grades. In addition, there were also other jujitsu schools that issued grades. Grades were issued up to 5th Dan based on ability.

The one big shock of the war defeat for Abe was the naming by the 'War Crimes Tribunal' of Japanese war criminals. At the head of the list was His Imperial Highness Nashimoto who headed the Butokukai for many years. Apart from this position he had no others. The Allies thought that militarism, imperialism, and ultra-nationalism had to be eradicated from Japan and they saw the Butokukai as being a hotbed of both. For that reason, they thought that its head should be indicted of war crimes and the organization itself should be dissolved. A week after the announcement, a picture appeared in a newspaper of Nashimoto carrying a bundle of belongings being led into Sugamo prison. Many Japanese who thought he was just a figurehead of the Butokukai were shocked at the photo.

Figure 60 Prince Nashimoto Morimasa was a member of the Japanese Imperial Family and a field marshal in the Imperial Japanese Army. After Japan's defeat, General Douglas MacArthur classified the Prince as a 'Class A' war criminal and arrested him (Wikipedia)

Abe thought so too and pestered his many Busen friends about this. However, they were more concerned about famine and national collapse and did not react to his arguments (Abe might have been one of the Kodoha – Syd Hoare). Abe argued to his former Busen colleagues that since the Butokuden building still existed, the Butokukai and its Busen martial arts college should be revived. Abe was not that diplomatic in his dealings with ex-Busen people. He had no organization, supporters or money and was unable to make his views possible.

He gradually isolated himself almost completely. Abe began to promote his petition to release Nashimoto and posted it up all over Kyoto, but nobody paid much attention to it. Many thought Abe was deranged. No Busen people signed his petition and Abe called them cowards. Eventually the fact that he was a policeman caused problems and he was warned by his superiors. The Butokukai tried to reform itself but the following year, both it and the Busen were abruptly abolished as was Budo education. Schools lost their martial arts facilities and many budo teachers lost their jobs. Isogai died, Tabata fell upon hard times and Kurihara ended up doing osteopathy. Abe on account of his contest record got a job with the Kyoto police as judo instructor. Many did not find any work at all.

Figure 61 General Douglas MacArthur held the position of Supreme Commander of Allied Powers (SCAP) after Japan's war defeat. In order to demilitarize the Japanese, he issued a ban on martial arts practice and abolished the Busen college (National Archives Catalog)

In 1948, the All-Japan Championships re-started after a seven-year gap due to the war. The ex-Busen judoka were treated as underlings by the grade issuing Kodokan. Eventually, this meanness became apparent. There were quite a few who sucked up to the Kodokan people. However, Abe refused his Kodokan 7th Dan grade.

In 1949, the Kodokan saw the abolition of the Butokukai as a good opportunity to create the All-Japan Judo federation (Zenjuren) as a national controlling body and eventually announced that it would not recognize either Dan grades or contest rules outside the Kodokan ones. Thus, a body was born which publicly gave authority to the Kodokan's advantageous monopoly. (see my 'A History of Judo' for a different interpretation – Syd Hoare).

Abe's preoccupation with reviving the Busen and the Butokukai continued. But he got increasingly bitter about his lack of support and vented his frustration on the Kodokan. He could not understand how the Kodokan could issue licenses and grades when its head Risei Kano, had never worn a judogi. Also, about the fact that judo practitioners remained silent about it. Abe strongly railed against this as he perceived it wrong. But in the process, he lost most of his friends and colleagues. Perhaps if Abe's wife had had three boys instead of three girls, he could have redirected his life into training one or more of them up to take on the judo world?

7 LIFE AFTER THE WAR

In 1946, Abe was demobilized with the rank of army captain and took up a job with the Kyoto police as a judo instructor. If he had carried on working for the police, he would have received a sum of money on retirement and a pension. He was a pillar of the Kansai (west Japan) judo world and there is no doubt that he occupied a position of authority in the Japanese judo world. He rented a house in Kyoto and was able to make a living for his wife and family. However, he gradually dropped out of sight and now (1986) not one of his fellow judo students from the Busen, or those who he taught, or even the Kyoto police had any news of him. They did not know whether he was alive or dead or where he was living.

(It was reported that he was spotted in Tokyo during the time of the '64 Tokyo Olympics but he had changed quite a bit. The author enquired among his old acquaintances as to his whereabouts. One said that he and his oldest daughter were making a living somewhere, maybe in the Tokushima countryside. Another reported that he was in an old people's home and somebody wondered if he was not dead. One theory was that since he was an eccentric character, maybe gone off the rails a bit. If he was still alive, he was perhaps not leading a normal social Japanese style life. – Syd Hoare)

It was about this time (early 1950s) that the famous Ishikawa returned from teaching in America. He met up with Abe and asked him if he fancied going to England to teach judo at the London Judo Society as someone from the UK had approached him about it.

Figure 62 Ishikawa (2nd from left) together with Sumiyuki Kotani, Kenji Tomiki and others during their trip to the US, instructing Air Force and Strategic Air Command members (Plaines, Charles Sr)

Abe decided to go for it and resigned from the Kyoto police. He was given a hearty farewell party. There is a theory that this job offer in London was rather convenient for all concerned. In London, he found lodgings in Brixton Road which was not far from the London Judo Society (LJS) dojo in Vauxhall. His landlord was an elderly Japanese by the name of Torii Kumajiro who had married a British woman. They had no children.

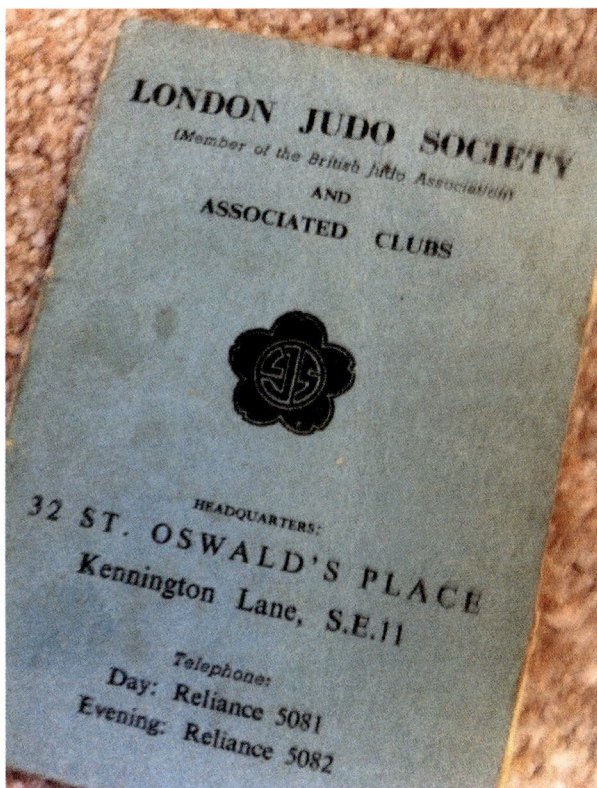

Figure 63 A record book of a student, John Gowland, from the London Judo Society (Jones, Paul)

At first, Abe was welcomed, and local newspapers carried photos of him throwing with Hanegoshi. But gradually, relations between him and the LJS soured largely, due to his possible eccentric behavior. At the time, there were two judo organizations in the UK. The main one (British Judo Association) was headed by Gunji Koizumi who had been residing in England since about 1906. The Kodokan regarded Koizumi and his organization as an influential base for promoting Kodokan judo and *"selling its Dan grades"*. Abe could not speak English but managed to communicate his passion for judo by his actions and gestures. Abe's students increased. But from time-to-time, Abe's views did not coincide with those of Koizumi and his organization.

If Abe had understood how judo was organized in the UK and had been more worldly wise, he could have been more courteous to the influential Koizumi and worked to spread his own message in his own dojo as nothing stopped him from doing it. But Abe did not think like that. As a result, Koizumi was forced to announce that Abe had not been sent by the Kodokan and was not licensed to teach judo. In opposition, Abe reacted by immediately setting up his own organization, the British Judo Council, along with Matsutaro Otani. At one point it claimed to have 3000 members. Abe tried to bring his wife and family to the UK, but his wife was opposed. The eldest daughter was about to enter middle school in Japan and the two younger daughters spoke no English at all. Abe's wife probably often had to disagree with her husband's suggestions and his somewhat unrealistic views. Abe's eldest sister Toyoko was 36 years old and was betrothed to a Tokushima man.

Figure 64 Abbe on the day of his arrival in the UK. He was welcomed by Eric Dominy, Matsutaro Otani and others (Taylor, Ross)

Abe continued to lose a lot of English support because of what was regarded as his eccentric behavior. For example, there was one occasion when Abe cladded only in a loincloth *(fundoshi),* jumped on a horse, and rode around a field in central London and caused women to scream. However, this seems unlikely. But there is an identical story of Abe riding a horse wearing his loincloth during a Judo course at the Bisham Abbey Sports Centre in the country. When Abe was Battalion commander of the Tokushima regiment, he often rode a Mongolian horse which was one of the symbols of the commander. Perhaps leaping on the horse was a nostalgic moment for him. (Eric Dominy who was one of the founders of the LJS told me that when Abe lived in the dojo when it was in Vauxhall, he filled his rooms up with many caged budgerigars and canaries – Syd Hoare).

Tokyo champion Watanabe Kisaburo of Chuo University Tokyo came to London to teach judo at the Budokwai and Renshuden in the 1960s. He occasionally went to Manchester where he happened one day to see Abe on the platform. He introduced himself but all Abe could say was *"Oh really"* and scurry for the exit. Abe, it seems, had little time for Japanese judo-men. But maybe he was surprised and did not know what to say or perhaps he was just a curt person. I managed to interview a number of British judo men who had been taught by Abe and they mostly said the same thing about him," *He had wonderful technique. His explanations were very good but...............?"*

Figure 65 Known for his unique style of Judo, Watanabe Kisaburo was an inspiration to many. Judokas such as Isao Okano, Brian Jacks and others cite him as an influence. Kisaburo was also an instructor at the Budokwai (Crowhurst, Stephen)

Relations between Abe and his new judo organization eventually cooled off. As a result, he bought a van and some judo mats and headed for Europe where he toured Marseilles, Nice, Monaco, Turin, and Rome etc, teaching judo wherever he could. Sometimes he rented an indoor space. At other times, he taught outdoors to adults and children and if nobody was interested, he took what other work he could find. He toured other parts of Europe and North Africa including Sweden, Algeria, Dacca. Abe gradually lost muscle and hair to the extent that none of his former students or acquaintances would recognize him. This was the man who enthralled 20,000 spectators at the Meiji Shrine with his phenomenal judo skill! Abe was not so good at making or keeping money especially in England where the English were strict with it.

Figure 66 Abbe in Italy with his student, Elio Lamagna to his left

Figure 67 Abbe teaching in Italy

Figure 68 Abbe instructing in a dojo at the invitation of C. Barioli (Croceri, Corrado)

Figure 69 Another shot of Abbe and Lamagna

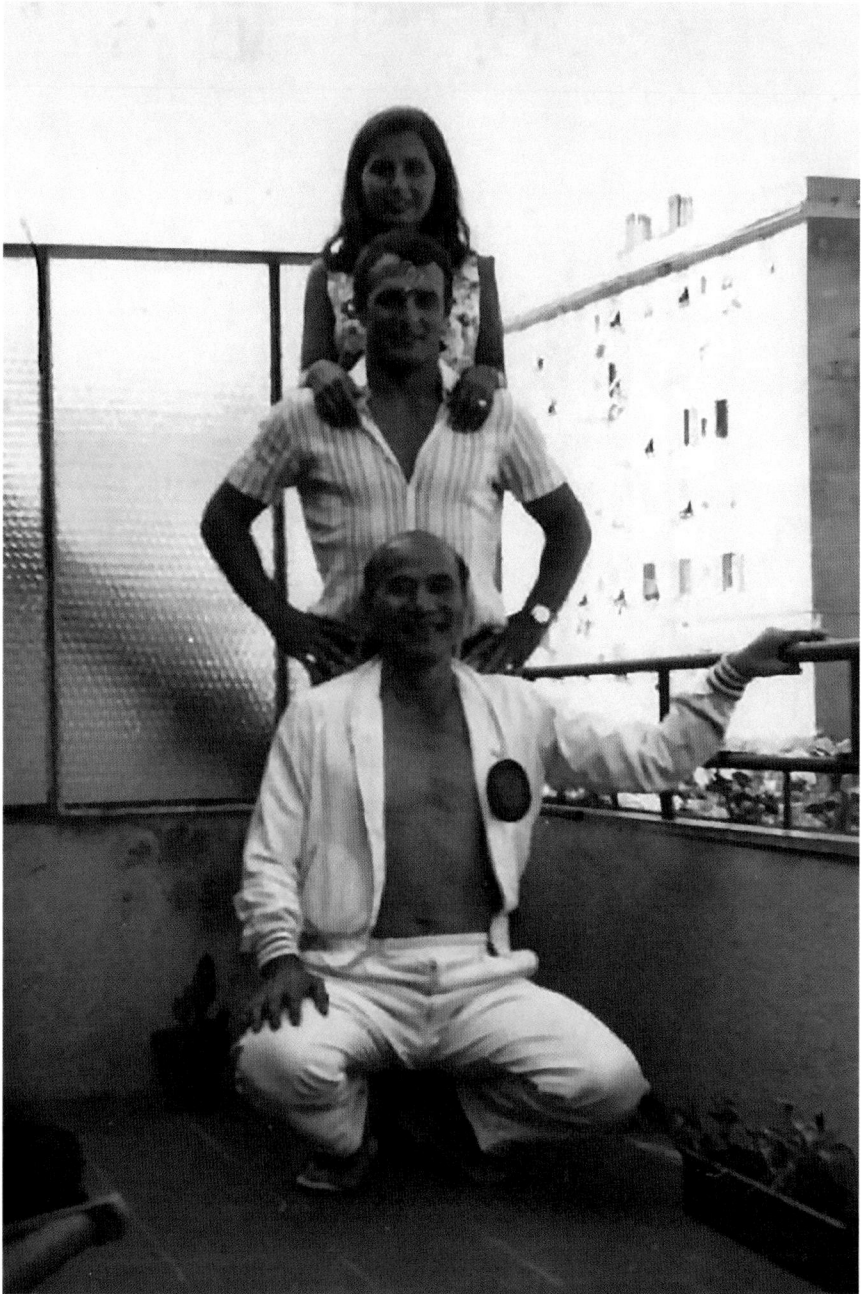

Figure 70 Abbe with Lamagna in Genoa

Figure 71 Abbe demonstrating ne-waza

Figure 72 Abbe demonstrating O-Guruma at Gothenburg Club, Sweden, 1959 (Taylor, Ross)

Nevertheless, he sent money back home to his wife and daughters and kept in touch at Christmas time and birthdays. When he first started touring Europe, he promised his family that he would only tour for 2-3 years and then return. But somehow, his absence extended to ten years. Then one day when he had sent a lump sum off to Japan, he confessed that he had nothing left to get him back to Japan. Mostly, he slept on hard narrow beds in cheap hotels. But there were strong clubs in France and elsewhere which used his services. Abe worked with Shozo Awazu of the Ritsumeikan university and with Haku Michigami of Busen where he got the respect he needed. It is claimed that both Michigami and Abe instructed Anton Geesink of Holland.

Figure 73 Shozo Awazu, together with Mikinosuke Kawaishi, led the development of Judo in France. He was well known for his expertise in groundwork (Alchetron)

Figure 74 Anton Geesink and Haku Michigami (Haku-Michigami)

Figure 75 Haku Michigami (bottom right), oversees the match between Anton Geesink and Akio Kaminaga at the Tokyo 1964 Olympics (The Asahi Shimbun)

8 FINAL YEARS

In 1964, Abe returned to Japan in time for the Tokyo Olympics where one or two reported glimpses him at the judo event. Then, he returned to his family home in Kyoto. However, his wife would not receive him, and he had little conversation with his daughters. So, he slept alone in a separate room. He spent his time between reading books, writing, and playing Go. Hosotani and other former Busen people heard that he was back and organized a welcome back party one evening. They gathered in a Kyoto restaurant. However, Abe did not turn up. He said later that he went out but could not remember the location of the restaurant. In 1968, his eldest daughter got married and both her parents sat together at the ceremony. But a couple of months later, Abe departed from Tokyo Haneda airport and headed for Brussels to continue his peripatetic teaching.

In December of that year, he returned to Kyoto again to promote the opening of a dojo in the Butokuden which he called 'Kyushindo' and to recruit members for his new mission, which was the foundation of the World Butokukai. The Butokuden was an incredibly old temple-like building that dated back well over a thousand years. It was in fact originally dedicated to the gods of war (Bushin). It still existed (in its rebuilt form) and had not been destroyed along with the Butokukai. Abe argued that since the Butokuden still existed, was it not natural that the HQ of ancient Budo (the Way of the Warrior) should be located there?

Figure 76 The Butokuden still stands today as the Kyoto Budo Center. In 1996, designated as an Important National Cultural Asset. It remains a stately architectural structure (Budo fandom)

It seems as if the war defeat, the dissolution of the Butokukai and the Busen martial arts school, and the post-war history of Japan had dropped completely from his mind. Just one theme ran through his mind. All he thought of was the resurrection of the Butokukai and resistance to the Kodokan. Like Don Quixote fighting the windmills, without permission, Abe set up his stall in the front garden of the Butokuden which was now owned by the city of Kyoto. His family drifted away from him and gradually, he lost what assets he had and was forced to move from Kyoto and into increasing obscurity. Few had any idea where he lived. However, I managed to find his eldest daughter and learned from her his address which was in a retirement home in Chichibu city in Saitama prefecture.

Without ringing in advance, I went to visit him and found him watching TV alone in a narrow room. His eyebrows had grown very bushy, and he looked bigger than the average 72-year-old Japanese. He did not appear to be troubled by my appearance. I told him why I had visited which he listened to, although he said little. He seemed interested engaging in a conversation. I asked Abe about the five-man match of 5th Dans at the Saineikan and told him what others had said about it. Abe said, *"No I was given lucky chance at that time. It is an exaggeration to say I handled him easily. Kimura soon became No 1 in Japan again"*.

Figure 77 Abbe, in the later part of his life

We discussed Yamashita Yasuhiro for a bit who Abe thought had retired from competition too early. Looking back on his life Abe said,

"My life in fact ended when I went on active service in the army in 1937. The forty years after the army were more from force of habit while I kept searching for that judo dream. As a result, my family suffered. It was the army that forced my severance with the Butokukwai and Busen both of which forced us to challenge our limits and ignite our youth. Finally, Butokukai and Busen were forcibly shut down and the Kodokan fishing in troubled water emerged as a monopolistic body with which I could not compromise. Somewhat different from my aims and ambitions I ended up searching for a new heaven in foreign countries where I tried to pass on what I believed in. One could say that I ended up having expended all my energy as a wandering teacher."

There was a sad echo in these words of apology to his family and as I looked around his narrow room, I noticed there was little in the way of household goods. I asked Abe if I could get him anything such as a change of clothes or a razor since he needed a shave. He replied simply, *"I don't need anything."* When it was time to depart, he grasped my hand silently. His eldest daughter Junko said of her father later that he was not a man to yield to the powerful. He could not resist kicking against the pricks. *"We are proud of him"*, she said.

On Nov 17th in the morning Abe went out for a bike ride with a neighbour called Goto. After a while, Goto noticed that Abe was not behind him and when he retraced his steps, he found Abe squatting on the ground looking very grey. He was taken to the nearby municipal hospital in Chichibu. He had suffered a major heart attack and died on December 1st, 1985, surrounded by his daughters.

9 KYUSHINDO
By Henry Ellis

I became involved initially in Judo in 1956 and Aikido in 1957 as a direct student of the legendary Budo Master Kenshiro Abbe Sensei. I was a student with Ken Williams Sensei at the now famous `Hut Dojo`. I am now involved with a few of the remaining direct students of Abbe Sensei in an effort to protect the legacy and proud lineage left behind by this great man of Budo, who was our teacher and mentor. It has taken a great deal of effort to collate the history and facts that we trust will one day be of benefit to future generations who will see through the fog of fraudulent claims by so many of some kind of association with Kenshiro Abbe Sensei in what can only be an attempt to gain some form of credibility.

Figure 78 The "Hut Dojo" in 1957

Figure 79 I was a student of both Judo and Aikido

The worst Kyushindo abuser must be the MayoShinDo group, who has made endless claims. The most bizarre of all, is the claim that the late Mr George Mayo is the founder of Kyushindo, a claim that is totally disrespectful to the memory of a great Budo master. I could not have achieved what has been done so far without the support of my long-time friend Gerard Gyngell Sensei, a sincere student of Abbe Sensei since his arrival in the UK. He was working in the London office of the British Judo Council (BJC) in the early 1960s alongside Abbe Sensei. In addition to this, Gyngell Sensei was in Abbe Sensei's 1964 Olympic Judo squad and a three-time Welsh Judo Champion. As one can imagine, a great source of factual information. Alongside Gyngell Sensei, I would like to mention Bill Woods. Both men played a great role in protecting his legacy up until their passing.

Figure 80 Gerard (Gerry) Gyngell in the middle (Jones, Llyr)

Figure 81 Abbe at his dojo with the 'Kyushindo' logo hanging behind

When writing articles such as this and others concerning the life of Abbe Sensei, fraudulent claims and facts are cross checked between our close associates so that we set the records of history straight. Sadly, we must accept that we cannot fight every single bizarre claim as they are on the increase almost daily. The only way is to promote the truth and expose the frauds by writing articles for the researchers that are genuinely interested in the truth. I can only hope that perhaps with our help, they will eventually find it.

It is not my intention to rewrite the history of Kenshiro Abbe Sensei. His life is already well documented. The purpose of this writing is to state that, 'Kyushindo' is not a martial art. It never was a martial art. Kyushindo was the life's work and study from the late 1930s of Kenshiro Abbe Sensei, who stated that it was a philosophy of his study of Judo, a concept that had made him the champion of the All-Japan tournaments and one of the few judokas to ever beat Masahiko Kimura Sensei. It was this philosophy that he tried so hard to impart to his British students. Sadly, he often despaired that these personal students could not fully grasp this deep yet difficult theory which had made him such a great Judoka.

We are saddened today to see so many people using the name of Kyushindo, whilst at the same time, intimating a connection with the name of Kenshiro Abbe Sensei. Now to the true purpose of this article. As stated earlier 'Kyushindo' is not a martial art, never was and never will be. Simply because it is a theory, or a philosophy as applied to Kyushindo Judo. We now see people claiming to be teaching ` Kyushindo Karate `. Let me make it clear, Abbe Sensei never ever applied his Kyushindo to other arts, only judo. Abbe Sensei has no association whatsoever with these people or their claims. One can only assume that the name Kyushindo was abducted and raped because it sounded so very Japanese.

It gets worse! There are people who are claiming to be Dan grades in Kyushindo! As much as I would like to laugh at the stupidity of it all, I cannot. As it so sad and disrespectful to the memory of our teacher. I recall Gerry Gyngell Sensei saying to me in astonishment once, *"Harry! how on earth can one have a dan grade in a philosophy?"* Having gone through the excruciating pain of traumatic heart bypass surgery, I thought that nothing could surpass such horror until I watched some so called Kyushindo Karate videos on Youtube. They were horrendous to say the least. I just trust that students will visit the great collection of Kenshiro Abbe videos on my YouTube channel before they accept that the *"Japanesy Kyushindo"* is the real thing. Simply type in *"Henry Ellis Aikido"* on YouTube to access the videos. I would not be surprised to walk into a supermarket one day and see boxes of *"Kyushindo Washing Powder"*. I joke without a smile as I can only feel disgust at the abuse of Kenshiro Abbe's name and other passed Japanese masters.

10 MEMORIES OF MY SENSEI
By Henry Ellis

The first time I saw Abbe Sensei was in the late 1950s at the "Hut Dojo". I was in awe of him then as I still am today as I write of his effect on my life to this day almost seventy years later. I was a member of the Judo section at that time. One evening, during what was a regular practice, randori session, there was a sudden stirring of excitement amongst the students. Everyone paused for a moment. I was surprised to see this Japanese gentleman walk in the dojo. Ken Williams Sensei gave a loud cupped handclap and everyone around me dropped as one in to kneeling position. Despite feeling confused, I quickly joined them. Then, we all bowed as one in respect to the Japanese man wearing a brown suit. I soon realized that this must be the already legendary Kenshiro Abbe Sensei.

Abbe Sensei spoke with Williams Sensei at the edge of the mat for a few minutes. Then, following the customary traditions, he slipped off his zori slippers before stepping on to the mat and giving a standing bow. Even though he was in a suit, I was amazed at how he moved amongst the high grades with ease. I had a distinct feeling that he knew how important it was for the students moral to feel the technique of such a master judoka. From that day on, and over many years, I

113

would no longer be surprised to see Abbe Sensei step on the Tatami in his old brown suit for Judo, Kendo and Aikido. We all referred to the suit as Abbe Sensei's *"demob suit"*. For those that do not remember the post-World War 2 era, when a British soldier was released from the Armed Forces, he would be demobilised and would go home in either a blue or brown ill-fitting 'one size fits all' demob suit. We assumed the Japanese army would do the same.

Figure 82 Abbe instructing at the 'Kings Cross' dojo

Abbe Sensei would occasionally sit with Williams Sensei and the students in the "Hut Pub". Although he preferred a glass of water, on a rare occasion, he may have a half pint of beer. I have read of people claiming to have chatted and drunk beer or whisky late into the night having deep philosophical conversations with Abbe Sensei. If one reads such stories, you immediately know the person is full of BS. Abbe Sensei's command of English was limited. Thus, a conversation would be difficult and time consuming. Moreover, he was a man of few words. I have told the story many times of Abbe saying whilst teaching, *"my English not good, my Shinai speaks fluently* "as he would tap the Shinai on the offending body part during instruction.

When people speak of their imaginary friendship with the early Japanese teachers, they fail to understand these teachers were often from ancient Samurai stock. They could be very severe, sometimes a little pleasant and rarely social. One could never get close to them as they kept everyone, I mean everyone, at full arm's length. As a result, one could never be familiar with any of the old style Budo masters. Philosophical conversations with Abbe Sensei; I never witnessed anyone ever try to get close or familiar with Abbe Sensei in all my early memories. Yet, one can now read of so many who now claim that either they, or their teacher were a close friend of Abbe Sensei.

A classic example of this unwelcome familiarity is a story I have previously talked about concerning Chiba Sensei. In brief, I was assistant to Chiba from 1967 to 1972, It was the first day of a weeklong 'Summer School'. Before the first morning session, Chiba privately said to me, *"Mr. Ellis, your discipline and etiquette is an example to all, can you please explain this to the students.* I asked *"Why, is there a problem?"* Chiba explained that the senior grades would call him Kazuo and put their arms around his shoulders like a dear old friend.

One does not disrespect a Japanese teacher in this way. I sorted the problem which did not go down too well with the natives. The familiarity ended there and then as Chiba kept everyone including me, at a safe distance.

Abbe Sensei would speak of his theory of Kyushindo and the principles of circular movement in his style of Judo. Kyushindo was never associated with his teaching of Aikido. Abbe Sensei was disheartened that no one ever truly understood his theory. I have seen where people who never knew Sensei personally have written of Abbe Sensei as being 'eccentric'. I never saw that; he was after all Japanese with different customs and values to westerners. Whilst most soldiers were only too pleased to discard their demob suits on returning home, Abbe was quite content to keep his. He was such a modest man and had very few items showing his success. His bedsit room at the large Otani home in Stuart Road, Acton, could not be more basic. He had a small TV and little else.

When Abbe Sensei was teaching, he had the ability to always have the full attention of all the students. I never knew one person who had been a student of Abbe Sensei who wasn't proud to make that claim. He was an inspiration to all that studied with him. Derek Eastman and I carried much of Abbe Sensei's teaching methods with us for the rest of our martial arts future. The discipline was, and still is, an important part of our teaching. The memory of Abbe Sensei will always be a part of who, and what we are. There are very few original students of Abbe Sensei left as time takes its toll.

Figure 83 Posing after a class

The British Judo Council (BJC), which he co-formed with Matsutaro Otani, had approximately 34,000 members in the UK and Europe. Robin Otani, the son of Matsutaro Otani, is still the president of the BJC which is sgoing strong almost forty years after the death of our teacher Kenshiro Abbe Sensei. He successfully continues the dream started in 1957 by his father Matsutaro Otani and Kenshiro Abbe to build a Judo organization that would promote their style of Judo to all students from all backgrounds. Robin Otani has proven to be a credit to the memory of both his father and Kenshiro Abe.

Figure 84 Portrait of Robin Otani

Figure 85 Matsutaro Otani at Grange Farm, 1966 (Witts, Len)

I have written of the awe that we young students were in of the presence of Kenshiro Abbe Sensei. I know that both Derek Eastman and I had similar experiences when first going into our places of work and excitedly telling everyone of our training with this famous Japanese Budo Master. Maybe we were just young and naïve and expected others to share our incredible experience. To my surprise, I found that many older guys turned against me for speaking so highly of a Japanese person, whom they despised greatly.

I almost came to blows with one of the guys as I tried to defend Abbe Sensei's character. No one wanted to hear my account of training with this great Judo champion. Instead, they were eager to tell stories of Japanese war atrocities in prisoner of war camps. My defensive arguments were totally pointless when one guy rolled up his trouser legs and showed the most horrific scars on his legs; they were deep and white, shiny almost. Being the calmest of all the people there, he explained being held as a prisoner of the Japanese. He further went into gruesome detail, highlighting that the scars were leg ulcers which were scooped out by a spoon that had been in boiling water.

I related this story to others the next night at the dojo. Apparently, this reaction had been the experience of many students. From then on, we learned an important lesson: keep our enthusiasm in the confines of the dojo. This hatred of all things Japanese carried on for many years. Even when I became a Dan grade and teacher, I would make a point of warning all new students to be careful of other people's reactions when speaking of the Japanese and the martial arts. Kazuo Chiba Sensei in his writings tells of the times he went to look for a flat in the Sunderland area, only to have the door slammed shut in his face once they realized he was Japanese. And this was as late as 1967.

At the 'Kenshiro Abbe Memorial Event' at Crystal Palace in 2005, one of the guest speakers was Mr Motai, the UK Japanese Cultural Secretary. We were surprised at the open honesty of his speech as he described how brave Abbe Sensei was to come to Britain in 1955 when World War 2 was still so fresh in people's minds and there was a very hostile anti-Japanese atmosphere in the UK. He admired how Abbe Sensei had overcome those difficult days and had done a great deal to improve relations between the UK and Japan.

Figure 86 Mr Motai at the memorial event

Overall, I am glad to have been given an opportunity to contribute to this beautifully written piece of work! I pay my respects to both the late Syd Hoare and my teacher, Abbe Sensei for their contributions to the martial arts.

ABOUT THE CONTRIBUTOR

Syd Hoare

The name Syd Hoare rings a bell among many in the Judo world. He was born in Paddington, London in July 1939. He started judo at the Budokwai in 1954 and trained under the famed Trevor Pryce (TP) Leggett. He immersed himself whole heartly in judo and did his best to reach his physical peak. Eventually, his training paid off as he became the youngest British *dan*-grade in 1955. In addition to this, he moved to Japan and submerged himself into the Japanese culture, even becoming a fluent speaker in Japanese. Hoare was also a member of the 1964 British judo Olympics team. Later in his life, he oversaw organisations such as the London Judo Society, the Budokwai and British Judo Association. He is noted for authoring many books on martial arts, which are still renowned to this day.

ABOUT THE CONTRIBUTOR

Henry Ellis

Born in May 1936 in Brampton, South Yorkshire, Henry Ellis is one of the last surviving pioneers of the now famous "Hut Dojo", located in the London suburb of Hillingdon. The "Hut Dojo" is well known for being the birthplace of British Aikido since its introduction by the late Kenshiro Abbe Sensei in the mid-1950s. Ellis has over 70 years of martial arts experience and has had the golden opportunity to train with many well-known figures in the Aikido world, such as Kazuo Chiba Sensei, Masahilo Nakazono Sensei, Masamichi Noro Sensei and many more. In addition to this, Ellis is the co-author of 3 books, where he shares his in-depth experience in the martial arts, *Positive Aikido, Founding of Jujutsu, Judo & Aikido in the United Kingdom* and *British Aikido History*. It is his hope that the legacy of his teacher, Kenshiro Abbe Sensei remains grounded in the history of martial arts.

ABOUT THE AUTHOR

I started training in martial arts, Aikido, from 2012. Ever since then, I have gained a huge interest in martial arts and also the Japanese arts. That led me to do intensive research and training into the martial arts. I will always be a student of the martial arts, longing to seek knowledge.

References/Bibliography

Sources

1) United States. Office of Education, 1906, *Report of the Federal Security Agency: Office of Education, Volume 2*, U.S. Government Printing Office. Available at: https://books.google.com/books?id=GRZRAQAAMAAJ&dq=tokyo+higher+normal+school&source=gbs_navlinks_s&redir_esc=y

2) John Horne, Wolfram Manzenreiter, 2004, *Football Goes East: Business, Culture and the People's Game in East Asia*, Routledge. Available at: https://books.google.com/books?id=ZuB_AgAAQBAJ&dq=koto+shihan+gakko&source=gbs_navlinks_s

Pictures

All images are copyright to their respective owners

Syd Hoare Dedication picture: *Syd Hoare 1964*, 2017, Tomizawa Roy, The olympians <hoare-passes-away-read-his-wonderful-book-a-slow-boat-to-yokohama/#more-13606>

Syd Hoare General Introduction: *Syd Hoare Budokwai 1970s*, 2017, Gallie Peter, The Kano Society Bulletin <http://www.kanosociety.org/Bulletins/pdf%20bulletins/bulletinx31.pdf>

Syd Hoare Signature: *Syd Hoare signature 1999*, 2014, Hayes Simon, Facebook <shorturl.at/bjmqK>

Syd Hoare Crystal Palace 1986: *Syd Hoare 1986,* 2017, Finch David Kanosociety
<http://www.kanosociety.org/Bulletins/pdf%20bulletins/bulleti nx31.pdf>

Figure 2: *Yoshino River Rafting*, 2007, Wikipedia
<https://commons.wikimedia.org/wiki/File:Rafting_on_the_Yos hino_River.jpg >

Figure 3: *Yoshino River looking east*, 2009, Paulman, Wikipedia
<https://en.wikipedia.org/wiki/File:Yoshino_River_- _Oboke_Koboke_looking_East.JPG>

Figure 4: *Yoshinogawa River from train*, 2016, Soramimi, Wikipedia
<https://commons.wikimedia.org/wiki/File:Yoshinogawa_River _from_train_of_Kotoku_Line_(east)_1.JPG>

Figure 5: *Amagoi Waterfalls*, 2009, Raggaeman, Wikipedia
<https://commons.wikimedia.org/wiki/File:Amagoi_Waterfalls_ 08.JPG>

Figure 6: *Kawashima Junior High School*, 2019, Cantabrio Asturio, Wikipedia
<https://commons.wikimedia.org/wiki/File:Kakamigahara_City _Kawashima_Junior_High_School_ac.jpg>

Figure 7: *Dai Nihon Butokukai Hombu 1932*, 2008, 文部科学省, Wikipedia
<https://commons.wikimedia.org/wiki/File:Butokukai_Kyoto.jp g>

Figure 11: *Kokushikan 1919,* n.d, Kokushikan
<https://www.kokushikan.ac.jp/100th/history.html>

Figure 12: *Kokushikan University,* 2005, Murata Takuya, Wikipedia
<https://commons.wikimedia.org/wiki/File:Kokushikan_daigak u.jpg>

Figure 13: *Tokujiro Shibata 1956,* 2014, Asahi Shimbun, Wikipedia <https://commons.wikimedia.org/wiki/File:Shibata_Tokujiro.JPG#mw-jump-to-license>

Figure 14: *Kazuzo Kudo,* n.d, Goodreads <https://www.goodreads.com/author/show/577644.Kazuzo_Kudo>

Figure 16: *Kurihara vs Ushijima,* 2018, Kodansha Ltd, Wikipedia <https://commons.wikimedia.org/wiki/File:Kurihara_vs_Ushijima.jpg>

Figure 17: *Tamio kurihara,* n.d, Judo Channel < https://www.judo-ch.jp/english/legend/kurihara/>

Figure 18: *Tatsukuma Ushijima 1934,* 2009, ポプラ書房, Wikipedia < https://commons.wikimedia.org/wiki/File:Tatsukuma_Ushijima.jpg>

Figure 19: *Shotaro Tabata,* n.d, Judo Channel < https://www.judo-ch.jp/english/legend/tabata/>

Figure 20: *Hajime Isogai,* 2011, judomododeusar <https://judomododeusar.wordpress.com/2011/12/ >

Figure 21: *1929 Tenran Jiai,* 2018, Kodansha Ltd, Wikipedia <https://commons.wikimedia.org/wiki/Category:1929_Sh%C5%8Dwa_Tenran_Jiai#/media/File:Sh%C5%8Dwa_Tenran_Jiai_Champions_in_1929.jpg>

Figure 22: *Busen College gate,* 2018, McCall George, Kenshi 24/7 <https://kenshi247.net/blog/2018/09/10/busen-and-koshi/

Figure 23: *1934 Tenran Jiai winners,* 2018, McCall George, Kenshi 24/7 <https://kenshi247.net/blog/2014/02/03/1934-tenran-jiai-illustrated/>

Figure 24: *Toyoko Abe and Kini Collins,* 2014, Amdur Ellis, Old School: Essays on Japanese Martial Traditions <https://edgeworkbooks.com/old-school/?fbclid=IwAR1v6hqmPD-qq53A3O_JQewj3OpdmDIJjPPKm5CBHbYPjVqrYAYP57wH_iQ>

Figure 25: *Toyoko Tendo-Ryu,* 2014, Amdur Ellis, Old School: Essays on Japanese Martial Traditions <https://edgeworkbooks.com/old-school/?fbclid=IwAR1v6hqmPD-qq53A3O_JQewj3OpdmDIJjPPKm5CBHbYPjVqrYAYP57wH_iQ>

Figure 26: *Heian Shrine,* 2018, KENPEI, Wikipedia <https://commons.wikimedia.org/wiki/File:Heian-jing%C5%AB_daigokuden.jpg>

Figure 27: *Mukden Incident,* 2017, Swift John, Britannica <https://www.britannica.com/event/Mukden-Incident>

Figure 28: *Hajime Tanabe,* 2017, Caligula Viva, Wikipedia <https://commons.wikimedia.org/wiki/File:Tanabe_Hajime.jpg>

Figure 29: *Nanzenji Temple,* 2009, 663highland, Wikipedia < https://commons.wikimedia.org/wiki/File:Kyoto_Nanzenji01s5s4272.jpg>

Figure 30: *Doshisha University,* 2009, ノーベル書房株式会社編集部「写真集　旧制大学の青春」, Wikipedia <https://commons.wikimedia.org/wiki/File:Doshisha_University2.jpg>

Figure 31: *Masahiko Kimura,* 2014, Ben, Lifejudo <http://lifejudo.com/2014/11/kimura/>

Figure 32: *Yasuichi Matsumoto 1948,* 2018, Kodokan, Wikipedia <https://commons.wikimedia.org/wiki/File:Yasuichi_Matsumoto.jpg>

Figure 34: *Emperor Showa at Saineikan dojo at the Imperial Palace, Tokyo, Japan, Jun 1934,* 2014, Chen Peter, World War II Database <https://ww2db.com/image.php?image_id=20238>

Figure 36: *Yoshimi Osawa 1953,* 2018, Kodokan, Wikipedia <https://commons.wikimedia.org/wiki/File:Yoshimi_%C5%8Csawa.jpg>

Figure 37: *Kodokan 2020 celebrations,* 2020, Bigot Patrick, Facebook <https://www.facebook.com/patrick.bigot.9/posts/10220810112266399>

Figure 38: *Masahiko Kimura 1940,* 2017, 木村政彦 わが柔道, Wikipedia <https://en.m.wikipedia.org/wiki/File:Masahiko_Kimura_2.jp>

Figure 39: *Sato vs Ushijima 1929,* 2018, Kodansha Ltd, Wikipedia <https://commons.wikimedia.org/wiki/File:Sat%C5%8D_vs_Ushijima.jpg>

Figure 40: *Kinnosuke Sato 1929,* 2021, 『柔道100人』 Wikipedia < https://commons.wikimedia.org/wiki/File:Kinnosuke_Sat%C5%8D.jpg>

Figure 41: *Tarao Uto,* 2017, Nishida Hiroshi, Wikipedia < https://commons.wikimedia.org/wiki/File:%E5%AE%87%E5%9C%9F%E8%A1%8C%E5%AE%9F%EF%BC%88%E5%B7%A6%E3%80%81%E4%BC%AF%E7%88%B6%EF%BC%89%E3%83%BB%E5%AE%87%E5%9C%9F%E8%99%8E%E9%9B%84%EF%BC%88%E4%B8%AD%E5%A4%AE%EF%BC%89%E3%83%BB%E6%97%A9%E7%A8%B2%E7%94%B0%E8%A6%81%E8%A1%9B%EF%BC%88%E5%8F%B3%E3%80%81%E8%A6%AA%E5%8F%8B%EF%BC%89.png>

Figure 42: *Koto Shihan Gakko,* 2007, Yasuoki Noguchi, National Diet Library Digital Collections <https://dl.ndl.go.jp/info:ndljp/pid/761459/8?contentNo=8&itemId=info%3Andljp%2Fpid%2F761459&__lang=en>

Figure 43: *Koto Shihan Gakko Kendo practice 1917,* 2018, McCall George, Kenshi24/7 <https://kenshi247.net/blog/2018/09/10/busen-and-koshi/>

Figure 44: *Jigoro Kano track and field team,* 2019, Meinaka Miyuki, Wikipedia <https://commons.wikimedia.org/wiki/File:Members_of_Track_%26_Field_Team,_Tokyo_Higher_Normal_School.jpg#mw-jump-to-license>

Figure 45 *Hiroshima Bunrika University,* 2009, ノーベル書房株式会社編集部「写真集　旧制大学の青春」, Wikipedia <https://commons.wikimedia.org/wiki/File:Hiroshima_Bunrika__University-old1.jpg#mw-jump-to-license>

Figure 46: *Shuichi Nagaoka,* 2019, Samurai Arts, Facebook <https://www.facebook.com/SamuraiArts/photos/nagaoka-was-born-in-okayama-prefecture-september-17-1876-he-trained-in-kito-ryu-/1241443079345460/>

Figure 47: *Jigoro Kano 1936,* 2015, Asahi Shimbun, Wikipedia < https://commons.wikimedia.org/wiki/File:Kan%C5%8D_Jigor%C5%8D_1936.jpg>

Figure 48: *Kyuzo Mifune,* 2018, Alchetron <https://alchetron.com/Kyuzo-Mifune>

Figure 49: *Takahiko Ishikawa,* n.d, Sharp Harold, Judoinfo <https://judoinfo.com/ishikawa/>

Figure 50: *Iwao Hirose,* 2018, Kodansha Ltd, Wikipedia <https://commons.wikimedia.org/wiki/File:Iwao_Hirose.jpg>

Figure 51: *Yamaguchi and Kimura,* n.d, Aikido Sangenkai, Pinterest
< https://www.pinterest.com/pin/193936327688327020/>

Figure 52: *Kimura standing lock,* 2018, Danaher John, Facebook
<https://www.facebook.com/2223789874572510/posts/kimura-when-you-mention-the-word-kimura-to-a-bjj-student-they-normally-think-of-/2248002445484586/>

Figure 55: *Marco Polo Bridge,* n.d, Seniram, World-War-2 Wikia
<https://world-war-2.wikia.org/wiki/Marco_Polo_Bridge_Incident?file=Marco_Polo_Brodge.jpg>

Figure 56: *Chinese sentry at the Lugou Bridge, Beiping, China, Jul 1937,* 2015, Chen Peter, World War II Database
<https://ww2db.com/image.php?image_id=23771 >

Figure 57: *Marco Polo Bridge 2005,* 2005, Hong Fang, Wikipedia
<https://en.wikipedia.org/wiki/Marco_Polo_Bridge#/media/File:Lugouqiao2.jpg>

Figure 58: *Kwantung HQ,* 2007, あばさー, Wikipedia
<https://commons.wikimedia.org/wiki/File:Kwantung_Army_Headquarters.JPG>

Figure 59: *Atomic bombing of Japan,* 2013, Levy Charles, Caron George, Wikipedia
<https://commons.wikimedia.org/wiki/File:Atomic_bombing_of_Japan.jpg>

Figure 60: *Prince Nashimoto Morimasa,* 2021, 富山飛行場建設委員会, Wikipedia
<https://commons.wikimedia.org/wiki/File:Prince_Nashimoto_Morimasa.jpg>

Figure 61: *General Douglas MacArthur,* n.d, NATIONAL ARCHIVES CATALOG
<https://catalog.archives.gov/id/6233761 >

Figure 62: *1953 US Air Force and SAC martial art instructors,* n.d, Plaines Charles Sr, United States Taiho Jutsu Federation
<http://www.ustjf.info/founder/founder_photo.htm#1953a>

Figure 63: *John Gowland London Judo Society Booklet,* n.d, Jones Paul, Paul Jones School of Judo
<https://pauljonesschoolofjudo.wordpress.com/history-2/biography-of-john-gowland-pauls-sensi/>

Figure 64: *Kenshiro Abbe UK arrival,* 2017, Taylor Ross, Facebook
<https://www.facebook.com/photo?fbid=10155164330881452&set=gm.505129246525118>

Figure 65: *Watamabe Kisaburo,* n.d, Crowhurst Stephen, Stevecrowhurst
<https://www.stevecrowhurst.com/backstory.html>

Figure 68: *Abbe in Italy,* 2020, Croceri Corrado, Facebook
<https://www.facebook.com/photo?fbid=10217069128055468&set=a.1042848466567>

Figure 72: *Abbe at Gothenburg Club 1959,* 2018, Taylor Ross, Facebook
<https://www.facebook.com/photo/?fbid=10155816559841452&set=gm.661902577514450>

Figure 73: *Shozo Awazu,* n.d, Alchetron
<https://alchetron.com/Shozo-Awazu>

Figure 74: *Michigami and Geesink,* 2001, Haku-Michigami
<http://www.haku-michigami.com/mononohu_3_e.htm>

Figure 75: *Geesink vs Kaminaga 1964,* 2016, The Asahi Shimbun, Getty Images < https://www.gettyimages.com/detail/news-photo/antonius-geesink-of-the-netherland-and-akio-kaminaga-of-news-photo/533015508>

Figure 76: *Kyoto Budo Center,* n.d, KAREL19 <https://budo.fandom.com/wiki/Kyoto_Budo_Center?file=Buto kuden_Kendo_Wikia.jpg >

Figure 80: *Gerry Gyngell,* 2019, Llyr Jones, Facebook <https://www.facebook.com/photo?fbid=10157101531544003&se t=pcb.849563355415037>

Figure 85: *Matsutaro Otani Grange Farm 1966,* 2015, Lenn Witts, Facebook <https://www.facebook.com/photo/?fbid=10153982768309358& set=gm.1663736667190203>

End

Printed in Great Britain
by Amazon